ab

Poet Twelve Vagabond Poet Tw

The Last Woman Born
on the Island

by Sharon Black

Vagabond Voices
Glasgow

© Sharon Black 2022

First published in September 2022 by
Vagabond Voices Publishing Ltd.,
Glasgow,
Scotland.

ISBN 978-1-913212-34-6

The author's right to be identified as author of this book under the
Copyright, Designs and Patents Act 1988 has been asserted.

Printed and bound in Poland

Cover design by Mark Mechan

Typeset by Park Productions

For further information on Vagabond Voices, see the website,
www.vagabondvoices.co.uk

Contents

For my parents, Ted and Dorothy Black

O wad some pow'r the giftie gie us
To see oursels as ithers see us

- Robert Burns 'To A Louse'

The Last Woman Born on the Island

The last woman born on the island

(i)

She's soft as a cot rag.
In the palm of your hand she's

a comma, an apostrophe, plucked
from a passage written in wool.

Tease her apart
and she's smoke plume,

a child's scribbled thundercloud.
She's a snag of sheep,

the kind bred for centuries
on the edge of the world.

Her stink on your fingers lasts
long after you've put her aside.

She's dark as night, as the pitch
into sleep, and the dreaming that follows –

a tide of remembering
most often forgotten by light.

(ii)

I'm soft as basalt, as a raven's bill,
a wreck, a rare find. I fall straighter

than you might expect,
from hand to ground, from sound

to silence, an all-seeing pupil
under a shut lid.

Coaxed apart, you think you see
through me, but all you see's

the other side: my heart's
in each particle, each cell

of the bright lump in the black chest
of the island I'm from,

the one you'll never find.
I'm nowhere, everywhere,

shedding sand
like grains of light.

After a Reading by Jackie Kay

From her lips, the word springs – *po-yim*
like a see-saw, or the Broom Park swings

we'd stop at after school, pumping our legs
until we were almost flying, leaping off mid-arc –

not yet aware of our place in the world,
not yet ashamed

of the way we spoke, of our city's reputation,
the Clydeside glinting like a flick-knife.

Po-yim – the way my mum pronounces it,
the rest of my family with no need.

At distant universities, we tried to shake off
all provincialisms, like shrugging off

a kissing aunt, or a thick tweed coat
we'd be buttoned into for the winter.

It went the way of gallus, clatty, shoogle, scunner,
and a donder up the Barras on a Sunday.

Po-yim, po-yim, po-yim – English friends
make fun when I say it. But I'm

salvaging the syllables, reclaiming ground,
filling gaps with clods of peat and gley

that smell of fags and steel and the burn
that trickled through the Mearnskirk woods

where we found that cushie-doo one summer,
fallen from a nest

and kept it in a cardboard box
and nursed it back to health.

Chickens

I love their clean good looks, their matronly demeanour,
the startled blinking as their heads poke
from the clapboard; the riffle of their wings,
their scratch and dance in grass; feathers damp
from midday sweat, their sweet and musty scent;
the sultry way the grey one's long comb falls
across her eye, the way the white one struts in front,
head cocked Ascot-high, wattle an oversize charm;
the staccato of their heads as they hear the donkeys' tread;
their scrabble for a scattered handful; the way they'll
polish off anything but onions and leeks;
their preference for pasta; their praise-giving for water –
heads tipping back to bless each serving;
their colourful vocabulary;
the way, when nervous, they yawp in unison;
the way they watch me watching them; the way this
makes me watch myself; the way the red one
hollows out a dry earth bowl and meddles herself into it
as if to make the point, which came first.

Eggs

This morning when I fetched the eggs,
our Sussex was still huddled
in the nesting box. As my hand slid under,
she puffed out, muttering,
shifting as if to leave –
but gently, slowly does it

and from between her silken chest
and bed of flattened straw
I coaxed first one egg then another –
milk white, butterscotch, umber, blond –
each unmarked despite the box's mottling of shit,
each warm and gleaming in my hand.

She looked surprised to see them,
wattle jerking to and fro, so I
lowered the roof, flicked the catch
and left her there to contemplate
all the miracles a day might offer up
in handfuls, at a stoop.

Made the Small Way

Leaves picked by strong brisk hands
in small backyard plantations. Wheels and hairspring
tweezered into place, the face

and bezel after. The lamp my husband
carved from one strong oak,
chainsaw coaxing spine and ribs

around the heart. Any source of pain,
any form of healing. Sunlight
on those tips of rhododendron, cajoling buds

along each branch. Islands. Silence.
A touchdown on the moon.
Ninety-seven miles of backpack to Fort William;

moors and peaty burns. *Achilles
tendonitis*. Any house down a dirt track.
The turning of the tide, the turning

of a key. Einstein's Theory of Relativity.
The whittled spindle on which
we revolve. Hand-written letters, phone calls.

A proper cuppa. Your smile
each time I stumbled past you on the train,
whatever you were writing.

The view of Kilchurn Castle on Loch Awe.
Things that last for seconds,
things that last for ages.

The book of poetry you lent me.
This empty pack of Fairtrade tea, its slogan, slipped
between the pages.

Tracks

A red deer ribbons through forest,
through a ragged pine-line

halfway to the sky. Sunlight pours
into green and copper bowls

and bright capillaries of snow.
Layers of beech rise up the bank:

all the years I've travelled here,
the skins I've shed.

A woman sitting opposite
predicts the lochs we'll pass:

Gare, Long, Lomond, Awe, Etive.
Then it's tipped aggregate

at Crianlarich, where for once
the train does not divide in two;

Lu's head on my shoulder, its soft
and heavy load; a sparrowhawk

skimming the underside of sky
carrying pieces of sunset;

bulging ewes, fit to burst
beneath its buttery glow;

a cracked red tub
in a flooded ditch –

the ways a heart can fill,
and empty.

Room Six

Not for me the clean sweep of ocean,
the Atlantic's glittering haul,
the sleeping bulk of Mull across the Sound:
give me this out-of-season garden
with its corrugated plastic greenhouse,
its broken trellis and the outline of a door frame
bleached into grass.

Last night when I unpacked,
cranked up the radiator, jammed the wonky door
shut with a spoon, I wished it were as easy
to fold away the lists, the end-of-term exams,
my husband's flirty emails to his students,
the forms and overdue accounts.

Since I woke, no one's crossed the lawn,
a crate of empties or kitchen peelings in their arms:
only this starling on a wire,
crisp against pale blue, which flies off
as I fix the curtains into place,
before I write him down, recording how his wings
bear off an oil-slick with such grace.

Passing It On

I bring my blue to the island.

I leave it along the path to the Community Shop,
the abbey, the graveyard, the new-builds and the Spar.

I lay it at the old stone cross,
scatter handfuls of it on wild garlic at the rookery.

The more I give away, the bluer I get.

I knit it into socks and scarves, paint it
into coastal scenes on canvas and on craft shop mugs.

One morning after breakfast I walk into the sea.

Nobody notices I'm gone.
Nobody sees the horizon breaking.

Lucky Penny

West coast, ten a.m., a table on my own.
Two young women, rucksacks,
edge-of-the-world hair, are chatting

over porridge. One wears a bandana –
last night, blue Aladdin trousers,
skin like autumn, dark spikes like an unlit fire,

she looked at me.
She sees me looking now, her slim arms
pausing on the place mat

as her friend sprays oats from laughing.
The sea behind is quiet, unrushed.
Sun ebbs on my shoulder.

A *lucky penny*, she presses it into my hand,
I'm passing it along. Her eyes are green
like bottles sent to sea, and steady.

She smiles like she knows everything –
turns, collects her rucksack,
ripples from the room.

The coin's worn, the Queen's face
is a Spanish peasant's, the portcullis
just a shadow. All the lives it's blessed,

all the reasons it's been handed on –
the way she vanished through the front door
like the echo of a gong.

Spoon

Shy concave, long-stemmed petal,
minted hull:
you scoop each thought

and turn it onto the page.
Upright, you're a circus mirror,
a topsy-turvy simpleton;

in your tray,
you're snug as an octuplet
or a lover cosied up.

You ferry soups and other sundries,
returning smeared with jelly,
furred with tiramisu.

Even empty, you serve up light
as if it were a medicine,
deliver it to our tongues.

Lismore

A ferry drops me on the tiny slipway,
stone hut for a waiting room, old red
phone box with a stash of maps.

Pictish broch, ruined castle,
abandoned lime kiln, burial chamber –
heritage centre, with a café.

Along a one-lane road, sheep blethering
on either side, mud tracks,
an occasional white cottage,

two Highland cows
by a corrugated shieling,
like copper henges.

Espresso?
The heritage centre's closed, love,
says a woman on her porch. *Covid.*

On Barr Mòr I lay my pack,
undo my boots.
Nothing's open here

except the sky, the sheep-flecked hills,
the face of that young farmer
when I stepped aside to let his tractor pass.

Heatwave

Through the net: a wheel of stars, a satellite,
the winking of an aircraft bound for Nimes.
Your hand in mine is hot despite a breeze.

From the river: the low hoot of an owl,
a screech and rustle on the bank.
All day I've barely said a word, each sentence

warped and dizzy, my voice
a stranger in my ears. Cassiopeia,
the Pleiades, Orion's Belt, the Milky Way –

I know the rhyme,
know the ones that twinkle
are stars, the ones that don't are planets.

I know the law of physics: the bright one straight ahead
might now be dead,
its light-waves travelling after.

Our daughter's sleeping in a hammock,
her phone still sending music
to her ears. I used to know

the names for all of this. You say *love*,
say *devoted*, say *desire*.
All I can say is, *look at all those stars*.

The Lean Years

I was a burnt stick, and a handful of paraffin.
An empty house; the yard at the back
where nothing grows. A winnowing shed.

I remember the deliciousness of *No*,
my whittled body, flesh an outsider,
the cult of bird-bones.

I gathered shells and stones.
The aching in my belly became a song
I'd known forever and I sang it loudly to myself.

It was the world seen through church glass.
I was bloodless and smooth,
an alabaster, useless clock.

I gulped air as if it were a reservoir.
My pockets were full of fish and they sparkled so brightly
you could see them through my clothes.

***

I remember blank days, blackouts.
Days I forgot names, forgot what names were for.
The revelation of one sweet clean drop.

Then a small bright pill –
Gone, the chest of snakes.
Gone, the restless doors, the plastic anchor.

***

I left my shadow in Sicily, draped across a chair.
I was eating swordfish and the last words
of an argument with my daughter.

My shadow didn't flinch as I stood and turned
and left it there. Sometimes I night-walk under streetlamps
to remember its feet hobnailed to mine

and I wonder if someone else is wearing it
or if it's folded in a cupboard, or gathering dust,
beyond the orange orchards, the high Sicilian sun.

Night Walk, Baile Mòr

Tonight, the burning line of gorse
on the southern tip of Mull is an ancient blade
carving up the darkness. Along the coastline,
the electric lamps of Fionnophort
blaze quietly in their small neat squares.

The Sound rolls up the concrete jetty, our feet
just inches from its silver
and I think about those five young men
one mid-December, boat capsizing
as they travelled home from celebration:
all but one, drowned. We turn

and walk between hotels and cottages,
the schoolhouse and heritage centre
where we pause – from the chapel drifts some jazz:
a young lad at a piano belting tunes
to empty pews, oblivious

to the faces at the window –
head bowed, hands jigging, chords and riffs floating
through walls of granite, gneiss
and leaded panes
to lose themselves forever in the night.

Fault Lines

Her voice breaks me slowly,
and the voice behind the voice. Yesterday she spoke
of the backs of hills,

of fish spines on a cutting block,
of promises and mirrors. Fasts and bread.
Today she speaks of waves

and the way *they* break, over and over.
I would like to be a kissing gate, the contact
breaking time and time again

at both lips of the semi-circle.
The people pausing as they swing the hinge,
shuffle to the other side,

the dogs on leashes, or running free,
weaving through behind them.
The strong bones on their way to summits

or to tend a tumbled wall,
vaccinate a calf, rescue a stuck ewe.
And the bones behind the bones, labouring

under all the weight of yesterday, tomorrow
and the places they need to be
or are simply passing through.

West Highland

If I were to lie back, this is the landscape I'd become –
blanched tussocks, copses of pine,
shining lochs, station platform signs translated
to a language I can't pronounce;

lazy fences, serious houses, two shaggy rams
by a pleated auburn stream,
alder, beech and dithery aspen,
Munros shouldering the lost weight of snow;

a blaze of gorse along the verge, pylons marching
over bog and moor, the ninety-seven miles we walked last year
with backache, slippery from sweat and midge spray,
the craic of good friends keeping us upright
as we lost and found the way.

Instead of gulls
(2020)

I bring you jays and woodpeckers.
Instead of Mother's Pride white sand

and turquoise bars, here are
lavender, wild thyme and leggy sage.

In place of Columba's Bay:
this shrivelled stream, that sunken river.

I bring you bitten fingernails
and scabs across my knuckles

where a rock got in the way.
Also weeding, homework, soap suds,

dead mice, chicken shit,
a henhouse that needs cleaning.

I bring you questions, pleas, refusals, favours
and my mother-in-law's interruptions.

I bring you a paler version of myself.
I bring you eggs.

Peace

rapped on the table and the world fell silent.
Peace was a stone, smooth and round, the size of an egg in
the hand.
Peace sat quietly as the reading began – one word, then
another, until
the room rang with a single voice, and a background hum
of other voices.

Years passed, people came and went, furniture collapsed
and was rebuilt.
Peace sat in a corner gathering dust.
Men fought and rose to power, coins were minted, plastic
swelled,
oceans were trawled.
Salt and *samphire* turned to *cuts* and *collateral.*

A soldier picked it up, rubbed it down and lobbed it into
the crowd.
Men threw it back. Children loaded it into rifles. Women
hurled it
at each others' faces as they stood buried to their shoulders
in the ground.

Peace became a word, became a statement, a fatwa, an
empty promise,
became a million burning books, a detonator in the hand.
Peace rapped on the table and the world fell silent.

Sheela-na-gig

She looks out wearing light
across the south end of the island. The chapel
is scaffolded, interlocking poles

rising thirty feet beyond the wall.
The opening on which she sits –
legs spread, labia

pulled wide –
is an arch of basalt and red granite,
weathered and freckled with sun. A steel rod

has been thrust through.
Fencing on the other side divides the view
into three square frames:

blue sky; two sheep on a grassy sill;
a skein of geese steering north beyond the abbey's
heavy coat of grey.

Fly

A trapped fly bumps and buzzes
but is no more trying to find a way out
than heather's trying to escape a mountain

by bursting up a trail.
It wants unbroken flight but bumps
because it doesn't know it can't continue

through a wall – or else wants
more light, craves it, is gluttonous for protons,
and fumbles on a pane

because it's aiming for the sky. It throws itself
against a surface, flings itself
again and again, because its instinct

is not to give up – to go on till it drops.
A trapped woman, what about her?
What makes her stop?

Cod Fishing, Firth of Clyde

We crawl beyond the shipyards,
past the Cumbraes, beyond the map's pale blue
to reach a darker zone. I'm twelve,

we're on a trawler – Dad, ten men and me.
Last week's accusation – *too old to play with dolls* –
still stings like salt-spray as I follow their lead,

casting baited line and tomboy bluster
over the edge. Ten minutes and my line jerks taut –
I drag and reel till silver breaks the surface,

lands thrashing on the deck.
Slam its head! I grab it, drop it, grab it,
heft it to a bench,

a gleaming muscle twice my forearm
struggling against my own,
and smash it harder than I've hit anything before.

I'd forgotten till now: the mighty head
slowing with each blow, the weight relaxing
in my hands, that wide half-bloody eye

staring out beyond the lifebuoys,
as a round of broad hands slapped my back
like I slapped that body down.

Ear

Biology, my favourite –
I'd copy the diagram, preparing for tests:
hammer, anvil, cochlea,
oval window, drum. I'd picture

a blacksmith at his furnace,
coaxing metal red then yellow-white, drawing it
like gum along the forged steel edge,
striking out hoe or horseshoe.

Then the cochlea, strange snail
suckered on a nerve stem, its purple shell
polished to a sheen, weighing up
each magnified vibration

which the blacksmith at the slack tub,
dipping iron, perceives as the waterfall
near his childhood home where he fished
for burbot in the millpond

on days he skived off school,
willow dawdling in the evergreen water
while he picked out songs
of blackbird, chaffinch, wren.

Landbound

Iona

Sprawled in the ruined nave, I pray
to the gulls, to the greylags arrowing overhead,
to the sycamore with its fat pink finger-buds,
to the cowrie shells on Martyr's Bay, to the dunes
and machair and the Atlantic's steady gaze,
to the serpentine washed up in nuggets, to the tight green balls
of daisies in their leaves,
to Sheela-na-gig with legs agape
carved on the nunnery wall,
to the historian overheard who analyses mortar,
to the multilingual starlings, to the language
of the sea, its mutterings and shanties,
to that streak of bird shit on the window,
to this astonishment of sun,
to the fisherman who doesn't speak for days
and the other on his doorstep mending creels,
to the dish of milk left out for strays,
to the Hermit's Cell and the causeway
leading us across the marsh from Sandeels Bay,
to our need for flight, for salt,
our hunger for fish.

Corvids

Marc Almond says their eyes are blue at birth
and when they die they return to blue.
I don't know if this is true but I've heard
they're clever, can fathom tools, can find their way
out of a maze. I know of a rookery
overhanging a thicket of wild garlic
where the birds laugh uproariously for days.
Once, a raven flew into our bath, floated
on the cooling water until I
fished him out. He hopped about our decking,
tugging on shoelaces, tugging on hems,
staring down the cats, before skipping
to the railing's bottom rung and tipping into flight.
On the electricity cable, he prinked himself,
watched us watching him. His eyes
were bitumen, melting in the afternoon sun;
blank, or full of understanding: Almond
doesn't say. Jays are rowdy neighbours, half-cut
petty thieves. Their wings are flashed with blue,
though I don't know if they hatch this way.
Almond planted a cherry tree in his back garden
as perches for his jackdaw, and for his body
and the jackdaw's to be buried underneath:
two blue eyes, two brown, settled
in the humus, dreaming in their beds
alongside sunken cherry pips,
the tree's roots drawing from their bodies
what it needs, conducting them
through topsoil into air as leaf, flower, fruit.

The Dream
Lewis, 1919

I dreamed him floating in the bay –
face to the seabed as if scanning
for grilse and charr. Knew it was him
from the red hair flailing, the shoulders broad enough
to thatch a house in a day.

Six weeks since the ship went down –
two hundred dead, the island a ghost,
in every house the curtains drawn,
buntings burned on the hearths, grouse and venison
left to ruin.

No news since those forty lads
were roped to shore, MacLeod on the hawser,
another forty lifted from the freezing water
twenty yards from harbour, night as black as peat-smoke,
so black you couldn't see

the upturned hull, the roiling surge,
the mothers, wives and sisters screaming
on the quay. No sign. At first we thought
he must be on the Skye steamer,
gone the long way round…

I dreamed him floating in the bay,
wind whipping up
the shirt dregs on his back, his body
smoothed basalt,
his arms splayed cormorant wings.

When they lifted his head his eyes were a seal's –
when he opened his mouth his song
was a humpback's, soaring across the Minch.
In his grip was a guttered torch, a lighthouse
guiding him home.

Angling

Two small boys point, open-mouthed, as minnows
throng, flipping out the water in their struggle –

now bigger fish are muscling in, pale undersides
catching the light, three large ones, rotating

round their meal like wheel spokes until
the bread slips from its hook

and drifts, jumping and plunging in turns,
taking with it

two small boys, in red striped shirts and matching shorts,
past the stone jetty, the orange floats,

the empty moorings,
far from the harbour wall, from the eye

of their grandfather stooped over his bucket,
fixing up another bait.

Collins Gem

A bird book sits on the table,
cover splayed and arched an inch
above its pages: a bullfinch

with its freight of sunset
grips a twig. This morning I woke
to my ankle pounding

under the sheets. No hike today –
I'm grounded, like the bullfinch
with its chubby beak,

its hairpin legs, its sculpted wings
glazed black and powder grey, tail
like two oars resting on a rowboat.

Sometimes I feel a sun might burst
from my body if I don't hold everything
in check. Or the thin line I stand on

might break beneath its burning weight.
A light breeze
makes the pages lift and flutter, the bird rise further –

the bound spine pulls it
back like gravity. When I die, I'll fill and brim
like this stack of printed pages,

arching over thermals –
then break free, like these grey-black wings
are meant to be.

Bystander

A three-foot weir,
a tyre churning water, grasping
for the mossy spillway

in a backlash of foam
like a small child
reaching for its mother,

slapped down over and over
while an uncracked mirror
carries the sky to its inevitable end,

the tyre once slick on tarmac
now circling midway across the Teith
until the rubber falls apart

or someone pulls it out
or a quirk of current
yanks it sideways.

Prototype

I make you out of wax and ash and strips
of lint unravelled to the floor. Make you taller
than any man I've made before,
curl you inwards like a foetus, no arms
in which to hold your half-formed head.

I make you in the image of my greatest fear,
give you a single lung, a single breath. It hurts
to pipe marrow into your spine, to sculpt
blades and ribs, to seal flesh
where your heart should be.

You make me out of need and quiet obsession,
twist lightning through my hair, place a half-moon
at my chest and throat, a knot around my arm,
acacias at my feet.
You make me out of questions –

how to conjure fire, noose a running prey,
smoke out a burrow or a hive
and melt the honeycomb thereafter?
I can't pronounce my name. You exhale
slowly into my mouth as if it held a flame.

Middle C

It's a fulcrum, a tipping point, the first thump
of a scale, the dirtiest white key;
it's two thumbs meeting – *How d'you do?* –
an arrow through its target, perfect symmetry;
it's a passing place, a kissing gate, a stile
between the highs and lows. The beginning
of a handspan, a pivot for every tune I ever played.

From a dog-eared book of farmyard songs –
green farmer's wife, green chickens,
green fence, green pail of thrown green grain –
I pounded through *Off To Market Here We Go*
while Mrs D sang, slowly and with pauses,
as I deciphered score to keys.

It was every weekday after school, before
homework books were opened, before *Blue Peter*
and John Craven, Mum listening from the kitchen
until I'd ticked off scales and études,
songs and preludes. That crotchet on its dash

became a lifebelt and a boathouse
where shame and doubt
were set aside while I whirled through the classics.
A place to pour my shyness into thumping great crescendos,
the pedal pumping and vibrating
until all I heard was silence.

Soon it was a perch on which to sit,
straight-backed and faux-impassioned, knowing
Mark Lewsey from next door was watching from the drive,
cigarette tip flaring while I burned, fantasizing
when he'd slide his hand inside my jeans
and I'd kiss that smoky breath
that didn't taste of Newton Mearns.

I closed the lid on Middle C just before my Highers,
old enough to Just Say No: other scales to climb.
Now the piano sits in a new lounge, a leviathan
shrunken to a pet, overlooked
and silent, its hidden ivories still ringing with those years,
that one note like a ball dunked in a net.

Hollows

Our house on Knowes Road:
the walled bed where Mum taught me
to weed, how not to

grab them from the soil
but sink the trowel, prise up the roots.
And how to tell

which were flowers, the signs
that one was there to keep,
the other an imposter:

the shape and size of leaf,
thick or fine, hairy or smooth,
what kind of head. I don't

know if I intended
to present them as a bouquet to Mum,
like Dad did with his

cones of cellophane
crackling with colour and scent.
Oh, the satisfying wiggle

as a clump gave up, soil
tumbling from its naked roots,
the dark rich hollow! I don't

remember Mum's reaction
to the double-headed dahlias
in my arms. I only know

when Dad returned that night,
his rage was thick with colour
and seemed to bloom from nowhere.

Monochrome

fresh-faced, almost porcelain:
    my mother slender as a beech wand
    in a lightweight rattan chair,
    a mass of permed curls, ribbed
    cardigan buttoned to the neck,
    white Capri pants revealing
    polished legs tapering to white pumps,
    hands clasped on her lap;

my father next to her
    in a wooden garden seat,
    white slacks, matching lace-ups,
    open collar under woollen V-neck,
    black hair slicked like Elvis,
    his eyebrows thick hyphens,
    already joining facts
    to argue, compounding even
    the simplest things;

my mother's eyes barely visible
    under all those curls,
    crinkling in a smile. She sits
    perfectly upright
    in the Glasgow sun, poised
    between a shadow to her right
    (coal bunker out of shot)
    his body leaning in her direction
    as if he needs her
    more than she needs him –

they must be twenty-one
    or twenty-two, at her parents' house
    in Campsie Gardens, no older
    · than my elder daughter now,
    children really, in black and white,
    their lives in colour
    just out of sight, like my grandfather
    with his Box Brownie, saying *Cheese*, stepping
    backwards onto the lawn.

Tobar na h-Aois

Difficult to return downhill after stumbling
upon *the well of eternal youth*. Behind the trig point
with views to Eilean nam Ban, we splash

our faces and our necks, stopping short
of pouring it inside Gortex
or jumping in.

The Atlantic scuffs our still-damp faces:
smiling stiffly, we joke that we've been Botoxed,
the mountain has a sense of humour

as we falter for the path, feeling our age
as a hip aches, a knee gives out,
the map goes flying. Far away our families

are busy with our chores, with texts and emails –
bank code lost, dog just died, number for the plasterer –
we flag them up, unanswered.

Picking through the heather, we juggle
those unfamiliar lives, tossing them between us
like balls we must keep spinning for an audience –

wondering if one fell, would the whole lot go rolling down,
would the mountain not look beautiful
in all those colours?

Things That Can Be Thrown

Voices from a stage. Knives
at girls spreadeagled on boards

Champagne against an ocean-going hull.
A cap above a surge

of heads. An opportunity
away. A pitcher on a potter's wheel.

A spanner into the works.
A first draft into the bin. Caution

to the wind. A lasso into air
to tame the wild. A wild card

into play. A lifeline.
A javelin to the far end of a pitch.

Confetti. A fist of silver
from a car. The trap below a sentenced man.

A coat around the shoulders
of the last one out the door. A plate

against a wall. Fire
towards the enemy. Hands up in dismay,

or higher, in surrender. A ring
into the sea. All of it, away.

Forbidden

This morning I am riddled,
my gut an out-of-tune violin
playing far into an unlit church.

I am not beautiful. I have scars
and calloused feet and my stories
are all limp-inked and soulful.

If I could cry like anything, I'd cry like this:
rock against rock, sky upon ocean,
sheet upon sheet upon sheet.

The White Cow
Callanish, Lewis

She emerged from the sea, udder fat
as a skinned sheep, the islanders thin as chaff –

said, *Bring your pails to the old stone cross,*
barely a skeleton itself,

where she stood, a white henge
at the centre of the ring, let them

draw their fill. Moon flowed through her.
Each night a bucketful for every man,

her hooves strong in mud, legs not ceding
to the milkweight.

A crofter with two pails arrived – *No.* Next night,
coaxed her dry.

On her hind hooves, she rose to her full height,
became a rudder –

seven tons of Lewisian gneiss –
of a ship invisible by day, like the one

that dazzled the island's young men
with talk of the New World

and eventually sailed them away.

Hebridean

Out of the ash
    steps a bruise
and another, now a mob
    helter skelter
into the eye
    of machair and sand, of marram and sod
until they come
    to the sea
where flames can be seen
    on far-off shores.
They shake the ash
    from their coats and their hooves
        and up rise
the scars and the bones
    of shepherds, spinners, weavers, thatchers,
boat builders, peat cutters and gull trappers,
    egg gatherers, net menders, fishermen. Up rise the broken
and the banished, in a single plume. And what is left
    is blacker than sleep.
Out of the ash step the sheep.

Gardener

A young man in the greenhouse
brushes down a shelf, a cloud of soil settling
at his feet. Seedlings wait in small black pots.
A tall shrub stands in terracotta.
He wears a blue hat, blue overalls
and a tidy calm expression.

I used to want to be a gardener –
to spend my days pressing life down into soil
and tugging life out of it. Once,
I harvested potatoes, sank my hands
to find the nesting clumps
and raise them to the surface,

each one a brimming golden fontanelle –
we laid them out in rows: they looked like infants
in a nursery, curled and sleeping.
These days my hands are clean. They knock
across a keyboard: the rows
of inky shoots and tendrils pushing up

from some mysterious gloom.
The gardener's face is creased
in concentration as he stacks his trowels
and markers, forks and shears,
carries a potted shrub
across the lawn and out of sight.

Every time I step inside

my bloodstream teems
with silver fish; red squirrels
spiral up the pines;
a roe deer dips her nose
into the bracken. Peaty burns wind

past slopes of scree. Without warning,
a pheasant rattles from my ribcage,
taking flight, carrying
its creaking red and golden cargo
low over the heather.

And here's the bog; the flock
of black-faced sheep; the field
of small, upturned, half-eaten neeps;
the splash of snow against a peak;
the stag prints in the mud –

and further in, a wall of birch logs
neat against a gable end;
the keek into a room,
its cast iron stove, its armchair,
tartan tweed, a woman stepping

through the kitchen, her smile
a lot like mine: a life playing out
against a backdrop of a bigger mountain,
taller trees, darker green; in the hall
my khaki wellies ghosted with brine.

Post Op
for Elisabeth

I spotted you this morning near Columba's Bay,
you sly rascal – before the climb
towards the slate grey loch, just past
that split in machair where beach pushes through,
past the lambs going mental as they
race us to the fence posts, player numbers
painted on their backs, past fat slugs
of goose scat and strewn button-top shells,
their smooth white spirals no bigger than tears,
their gently wound mysteries –
in a hollow to the right, a sheep,
shaggy and wise, with high Finnish cheekbones
and an aquiline nose just like yours –
standing, staring straight at me
with two lambs suckling, one on either side like wings,
tails frantic as propellers: a light aircraft
flown in from the recovery ward
to watch our pilgrimage,
blessing each of us in turn as we
made our way to the pebbled bay
at the south of the island, the Atlantic
winking like a waggish aunt,
the mad scrabble for green serpentines
of which you are the queen.
I didn't find a big one, not like yours, but a handful
of smaller, speckled stones like eggs
that I tucked inside my clothes
and carried back across the peaty scars
and the new wood bridge
to the sill of my hotel window with its perfect
view across the Sound.

Eriskay Wives

On clear days, the Minch
is a navy gansey laid flat to the horizon:
a downturned palm can almost feel
the warmth of a man's chest,
his heartbeat.

When wind swoops in, nudging
sacks of herring meal, stacks of peat
and creels pulled clear of the water's edge,
the sea's a rumpled sleeve
of plain and purl.

It's the other days – when even gulls
and kittiwakes take shelter
when door frames yowl and stone weights
stutter on the thatching –
that the island holds its breath:

stars are guttered lanterns, clouds are hulls
and rain threatens
    to unravel
the rows of knitted panels –
horseshoe, starfish, anchor, net –

it's then we fetch our yarn, keep
our fingers busy
with a gansey for the eldest, for his brother,
for the youngest on his way,
the click of whalebone our covenant

that as long as we're still knitting, the sea
can't take them, the thread
between us can't be lost,
five-ply passing through our fingers
from the deep skeins on our laps.

Plea to Boy on a Train

Small boy with your camo fleece, your crochet
and your bag of wool –
turquoise, rust, grass green, magenta –
your mother beside you with her wool,
laying down hers to demonstrate a stitch, a loop,
without making a lesson of it –

remember the brush of ply
against your wrist, the needle's cool,
her undemanding arm against your own, the hook
that lifts and rescues, feeds and anchors
one thread to another, one row to the next, each stitch
an eyebrow raised in permanent question.

First Keys

Up two dirty, spiral flights:
a box room with two hobs, a sink,
a shower head without a dock, its rail

held up by washing line and in the tray
a gecko she names Norman.
I push the sofa into place, empty crates

and make her bed, kick a concert flyer
from my sole; spot the mortise, deadbolt, nightlatch
on the door and the peep-through gap

beneath it. I've seen the notice in the stairwell:
*Due to recent burglaries please keep
the street door locked –*

she hates me fussing so I tend
to Norman, stock-still even when
his head is stroked, his sucker feet are nudged.

Later, with a kiss, I say have fun
and don't forget to feed him, give him water, shade,
make sure he isn't trampled.

Celia's Shoes

are yellow patent, high-heeled,
abandoned on the gallery floor

before a painting of an inlet
flecked with shadows

like the iris of an eye, like a green stag
bucking under blue antlers –

as if she'd lost herself entirely
in the ocean's ebb and flow,

the lapping of her blood, its shingle
polished smooth;

as if she'd eased her feet free
and dived right in –

leaving us to wonder
at the hug of limestone,

the tug of a sable brush
in a calanque's undertow,

the way light falls on
the water's shoulder, just so.

Thirty-Seventh View of Mount Fuji

A young woman sits, straight-backed
in a loose silk patterned dress,
skirt hiked up over one thigh, her right hand
holding it in place.

No one knows how long she's been here, or why,
though some say when she arrived
she was a rice paper screen
but over days and weeks she opened like a lotus.

A strand of black hair drifts across her face,
her eyes are half-closed, her skin gleams
under halogen,
her lips are slightly parted

like the blouse of her wraparound dress,
her cleavage etched in shadow
as, against the window,
night presses in.

The artist, slightly hunched, moves out,
moves in, dipping and lifting his palette,
drawing his brush across her cheekbone
like a cloud across a summit

or the final stroke
to the kanji symbol for *desire*.

Death Trumpets

breathing rock   they are
delicate dark bouquets   stormy bundles
near the stream   a cluster of dark throats as if
shadows were tuning up
not death but   flesh risen from death
each mouth singing singing –
brush aside
chestnut leaves   leaf-mould   moist earth
there are more –
in your upturned hat
a nest of inky shavings   to simmer later
with cream and pepper
a garlic clove   some wine.

Twelve

I fear open doors,
translate night by the jangling of its stars.
Listen. That's rain talking;
sky shaking out its hair;
the walls of an icebox relaxing.

Every day, my father turns away.
Every day, my bed is a field where I lie down
one last time.
My pegged pants burn like flags.
In the kitchen, my mother can't sit still.

I crave unbreakable air. We're on a train
and sunlight is a cat's hot paws on my lap.
The track drifts on and on like water.
We sit in lines:
fresh eggs propped upright in their tray.

Recipes

Door unlatched, we'd push our way –
satchel, blazer, gym bag –
into sugared clouds of fruit scone,
buttered crumpet, Danish pastry.
Welcome home, girls! As we ate,

she'd empty the dishwasher, empty our heads
of geography and maths with news
of Jean's botched perm, Pam's new boiler,
Janet's winning bridge hand,
fluttering between cooker, sink and fridge

and chopping-up for dinner: cock-a-leekie,
neeps and tatties, fish pie, clootie dumpling,
tending them with chit-chat, song –
Lloyd Webber, Sound of Music, Dolly Parton –
supple, radiant, a voice she could

have taken round the world
but kept for us. A ribbon, it unfurled
from deep within the kitchen
and into every room.
In summer, windows open, her songs

rang from the house
and down the drive. I often wondered
if she sang when we weren't there,
crooning love songs to a bowl of lentils
or a pan of sautéed onions.

She was standing
shelling peas, shoulders shuddering,
hand wiping a flushed cheek, reaching for
a crumpled tissue on the counter. Said a speck
was in her eye. I didn't ask her

what was wrong, just retreated
from the room, too young to fathom
this new feeling in my stomach, too old now
to lift the foil on that strange recipe
whose ingredients I can only guess.

Upper Cut

Across the street my daughter's
hair's being cropped,
dyed postbox red – to mark
her first period.

My silver pot of tea's still brewing.
I nurse the empty Café Bibal cup,
the too-small handle,
the red stripe down the side.

Earlier we picked out bras – replacements
for her starter size – impossible to find
one not underwired, or padded,
not bolstered for cleavage.

She sits at the mirror, tilting her head
this way and that so the fringe
falls across her eyes
in a way she knows is sultry –

the stylist, all in black, his face
amok with piercings,
fusses at her nape, blades flashing,
and, moving sideways, perfectly conceals her.

I take a last sip, order another.
The waitress brings an identical silver pot,
the same cup with a red stripe down the side,
the same too-small handle.

Fourteen

If only good times passed more slowly.
It makes sense, she says,
darting to her laptop from the sink,
the fat and pearly soapsuds heaving,
popping on the white enamel.

She pulls on gloves, scrubs a sieve.
Fever Ray's percussion slinks
across the counter, a sudden updraft
lifting a bubble from a grater, cradling it
towards the window.

Cos they're the best ones,
we should make them last. The bubble
plants itself on the glass,
turning pines and mountain
upside down, adding a rainbow.

Her hands glide through the water,
find a saucer, wipe it, turn it round
and stack it on the rack.
Take last weekend, she says, a spurt of sun
picking out the sud, firing it with light.

Jack was here for two days,
it only seemed like one – then back to school.
She rinses off a plate, plumps the knives and forks
like wildflowers in a vase.
You listening?

The lifespan of the bubble hangs
between her hands and the kitchen pane,
its held breath fading
as pine trees and mountain
and half a neighbor's house are sucked

back where they came from –
she pings the gloves off, drops them,
pulls the plug to drain;
just a round stain, barely there,
between sill and lintel.

Seventeen

She films the milk
in the miniature jug, houseflies crawling at its rim,
films the swivel fan and her camera's reflection
in the window; me splayed heat-exhausted in a chair.
She wants to write a script at the end of her exams
before taking off to travel. She wanders

past the buddleia, bleached orange tips erupting
from a green sequined bandana
over bare face, freckles, spotted T-zone,
razored T shirt and cut-off jeans with the pockets hanging
    down,
legs unshaven because to do so
would buy into the patriarchy.

The aperture widens, the lens zooms out:
Grandma deep in paperback romance;
Dad frowning at his laptop; her unpacked suitcase
in the courtyard, painted DMs dangling;
the low sun picking out the trellised vine,
its gnarls and knots, its early-summer leaves.

She turns the camera on herself,
tells the lens, *Everything is art*, palm upturned
as if catching each word as they fall
to stop them slipping through the decking,
getting lost among the weeds
that none of us have cleared.

Urination For Girls

Mornings are a rush:
the bladder's quick release,
last night's wine or water
a golden gush accelerating hard
speeding down
the main road before
purring to a halt.
Outdoors is best. Crouched
in long grass, that deluge
into soil can make a woman giddy
with its rightness:
the blunt and hot necessity,
the nutty vapour
rising like an aura
above the steam.
Misjudged, an ardent piss
can soak a shoe,
saturate the pants,
leave her with a nettle rash
or a gusset full
of burrs.

But better a woman's surge
than a man's dejected arc,
one hand on his limp
and slug-like cock,
a single braid of pee
showering the grasses,
or a toy gun firing
machismo at the wall,

slurring slogans onto brickwork, tarmac,
competing with his pal
behind the Rose and Crown
who can hit the furthest point,
the sputter, halt and
sputter till it's through.
No, a woman directs herself
straight down into soil,
genitals just
inches from the surface
the stem of her so strong it could lift her
like a gorgeous lily above
a flowerbed of dew.

Cusp

Up a path that's barely there, jostled
by heather, holly, low-lying oak,

the child I was, shy and furious, is trying
to fight her way out. The twenty year-old

is fighting herself, frightening her parents
with an alien hunger. The studious teen

slumps darkly. An athlete the same age
has wings on her feet, a basket of snakes in her head

and in her stomach an empty fridge
which takes up all the space.

There's the new mum, thin and jumpy;
the journalist gulping cheap wine

from a bottle she offers round. The wife declines
another glass. The poet takes up

little space, barely more than a light bulb.
I reach the wooden footbridge

and in the water watch my mother
and my father until they're in their parents' arms,

each embodiment rippling outwards
as a new face seeds another flower.

Up through loose shale, I reach tarmac, unzip
the bag, and let them all out. The view

is long and deep. *Not quite what you expected*, I say,
as off they trot into the future.

The Left
is in George Square, red asphalt
mobbed by doos and chucked crusts,
dondering round the plinths of Walter Scott
and Rabbie Burns, round the benches
with their scunnered mums and weans,
the couples sharing pokes of chips, the old boys
with their caps and sticks, overlooked
by Queen Street Station's stream of cases, trolleys,
brollies opening like flowers,

dangles above the Clyde,
a slo-mo seen-it-all dawdling
past the Finnieston crane, criss-cross jib still reaching
for a cargo that never comes,
past the Armadillo, past the concrete girders
of the Kingston Bridge, around the Renfrew Ferry
where Friday nights we'd strip the willow,
dash the sergeant, reel and spin to pipes
and fiddles, givin it laldy, until the place was hoachin
and our balance went to pish,

shuffles in a queue in Safeway, Byres Road,
among the students and the hippies,
the yummies and the yoga teachers, the ones
who're swaying, skint,
and haven't got a scooby,
eight check-outs, Irn Bru, Lorne sausages, oakcakes,
Tennent's six-packs,
flavoured vodka, ciabattas, cheeses all the way from France,

et

The Right
is in Place de l'Eglise,
limestone paving round the fountain
with its brass fish spouts,
twin bars either side on which to rest
a bucket or a *bidon*, overlooked
by blue hydrangeas, vines,
the boarded-up Café du Nord,
the shy Hotel Bourgade, tables spilling
to the *boules* pitch under leafy planes,

shivers ankle-deep
in the Gardon's green mint chill, the weir
we jump from when we're brave
into the glass-bottle *gouffre*
from which we scramble
to the rock below the *cascade*,
pull ourselves to standing,
shout in stutters
as white tonnage
pounds our spines,

stands in Frank and Val's *épicerie*,
warm croissants, sugar-dusted *chaussons*,
pains au chocolat, golden baguettes,
Sylvie's eggs, Valérie's sweet onions,
chestnuts, honey, almond *sablés*
from Claire and Alain at Le Folhaquier
soft moons of goat cheese
stacks of *Midi Libre*,

is scuffing up the floor
in Nice'n'Sleazy, the DJ
pumping grunge and indie,
then upstairs to the bar
for a swally of whatever
and onto Reds, a snog and fumble,
blootered, staggering
over Charing Cross and back to Maryhill,

muddies up at T in the Park, 1994,
One Dove, Björk and Del Amitri, the boys
all shirtless, peely-wally, aff their heids,
the tents all heavin,
the portakabins mawkit, swimmin with puke
and jiggin to the beats,

steps from a red sandstone tenement,
one bed flat in Shakespeare Street,
a twenty minute walk to Hillhead tube,
past the BBC, Botanic Gardens, Oran Mòr,
then a bigger flat in Woodlands
with its Gaelic School, its mosque,
its wafts of cumin, clove and coriander,
its shops of bhajis, flatbreads, ladoo, barfi,

strides in a lace-up DM,
black and knackered,
from Schuh in Sauchiehall Street,
tight leather round the ankle
that always gives a blister
when storming up Byres Road
after work, the tube from Central

draws circles in the air in Seb's café,
its orange and yellow parasols,
plastic chairs, his panting collie
wandering around our legs,
its pastis, Orangina, Pierre M's home-brewed beer,
the tourists in the summer,
the *chasseurs*, *pêcheurs*, *ouvriers*
all year round,

potters round the Festival du Tripe,
bowls of watery soup, *degustations*
courtesy of the Alès tripe guild masters,
brass band, mayor's speech,
Bernard flipping *galettes*
stuffed with *pelardons*, *confitures*,

steps into a former silkworm farm
schist, refurbished, on the valley floor
a mile outside the village,
mulberry trees still fruiting
in the long-abandoned field,
whose leaves were gold
to *paysans* raised
on sweet chestnuts, milk, *lardons*,

sweats in a Vibram sandal,
black, tough, supple enough
to climb the mountain
on the *sentier du champignon*
to post a letter
collect a daughter
from the school bus, walk her

into Hillhead, a slug at Jinty's,
then another, then the dancin
and the walk home after dark,

shelters at the bus stop
outside HMV in Renfield Street,
a Saltire blethering
from a top floor sill,
its white-on-blue diagonal cross
going mental in a baltic wind
like a loose page of the *Evening Times*.

back along the road,
past wild cherry trees she shins up
to gather a skirtful,

hesitates on the sill
of the *St André mairie*,
a Saltire blazoning a plaque
between the flags above the door where,
footering with paperwork
for dual nationality,
I cross the threshold with my dossier.

Trefoil

Twenty years have shrunk it,
blurred it, faded it to blue:
a Celtic knot to symbolize
the many loops of love, its endless weave
inked on my right shoulder.

It was sunny, hot for June,
some place near the Trongate,
a pane between the studio
and the crowded waiting room:
a thin guy, can of Tennent's, off his face,

another there to switch the letters
in script below a Gothic heart.
You chose an *Om* on your left hip,
went first – rolled down
your jeans, leaned forward,

smiling through the glass.
My turn and the needle burned, a skean dhu
blazoning outline, colour.
Agony, you later agreed.
You might have chickened out.

This mark of our commitment:
creased, flattened by the years, it looks
more like a cross-legged Buddha,
or a spaceship, hovering, recording
all the ways we bring on tears.

Love

Its face is slightly misaligned,
is pocked and scabbed,
has spider veins. It bears a scar

where it was twisted
from the mould of every love
that ever was. You might feel

its breath on your neck
but you won't hear
what it's saying.

It rings its own tongue like a bell.
It begins your name.
It is a snake. It wriggles

from its skin: a dropped stitch, a kink
in an unravelled knot.
Stupid, solitary,

it's a short-stemmed rose.
They say it's almost worthless,
a pouch of ancient cowries

yet love contains the sea, writes songs
and suicide notes. It's a rope
ladder, leading

to a childhood fairground
with its dodgems
and its hall of mirrors. That face.

I would have liked

to be a girl, perhaps a snail.
to swallow the world.
to rename my fury and call it a giraffe.
to reach those tenderest leaves,
and to have nipped them from the sky.

to remember mouths,
my lover's especially, more succulent than any fruit.
for my hand on his to be steady as an acacia bough
despite the desert winds.

for elephants to trample
my ribcage, the bones and all the voices in them
brimming with sand
while the rest of my body surged ahead.
I'd have liked to remember the journey.

I know I travelled by foot and people
tried to stone me as I passed.
I'd have liked to leave behind
the dusty workings of my heart.
This wasn't the landscape I'd dreamed of.

I'd have liked to gather in my pockets
the stones of all those years
and to have one day built a house with them.
to spend my time in shopping malls, at parties.

I have buried my soft body in the land's skin:
the bright stones and the black clay,
the rich loam
and the packed ice, blue and gleaming
as it slides its inexorable way home.

Her Hair

It rises as she cycles, a brown scarf
stitched to blonde, a stash of rippling
ice cream, a vanilla/coffee contrail.
It was postbox red then blue
before the colour lost itself
to shampoo, heat and ultraviolet. It lifts
at both sides, bleached strands
surging up like wings, or a flight path
more than bird or plane or angel.
She's flying down the street
like she's flying into life, feet off the pedals,
legs stuck out beneath the charity shop
skirt, flamingo socks and T bar Docs.
She wants to grow it to her ribs,
it hasn't been that long since she was twelve.
I want to run my fingers through it
but she'll never let me. Sometimes
when we hug, I turn in to her neck, inhale,
like I did when she was young, drinking
milky sweetness, heavier now
and tinged with sweat.
She ties it up in quick elastic
and blonde drizzles down like icing;
she knots it into space buns
and looks like her first teddy. But today
it's swaying free, she's off her bike
and leaning on a railing, looking at
the anchored yachts in the marina,
a tanker in the distance, the rocks
between the pier and quay, the breakers.

A Seat at Cailleach Farm

(i)

She lumbers over marsh and machair –
coat tail flapping, stick feeling the way.

Ewes huddle by a five-bar gate.
An empty bucket rattles on a post.

The farmer's truck is absent.
The pier is empty, the dirt track too.

Only the gulls bear witness as they curve
above the fields, the pebbled yard

with its wooden bench, a brass plaque
engraved *Cailleach*.

(ii)

Don't cover me in winter
while the barn owl's roosting,

the white heart of its face
dipped to its chest. Let me

be adrift in a bog of flag irises,
sun in my throat

and earth in my voice. Let me
take it in, in huge gulps

and then in sips. Let me lift
the soft bright wings of darkness to my lips.

(iii)

She walks and walks, her basket
spilling boulders that roll

to the sea, boulders big enough
to land a boat on, build a home.

On they tumble: basalt walkways,
cliffs of gneiss and tuff, granite columns

landing upright. From time to time
she takes a chisel

and tames a fallen rock in the image
of a hare, gannet, weasel, otter, eel.

At the bay, she tips the remnants of her cargo
into the Atlantic: stepping stones

that will be named for islands
when the animals break free.

Revisiting the Island

Mull is rain, a washed-out sky,
the gorse's yellow flames long guttered.
I'm already lost.

The waterhole is dark brown
flecked with white, I don't know how deep.
They say three feet but my thoughts

don't touch the bottom.
Monks stitched speedwell
into their hems

before they walked a pilgrimage,
now the bright blue flowers
grow along old pilgrim routes.

If this path leads anywhere
then let it bring me loss along the way,
a letting-go of this hard pack,

a setting-free of names.
Dropped seeds.
The island gives me

everything I need and there's nothing
I wish I hadn't said:
everything was true.

But I wish I had said sorry.
I wish I'd said goodbye.
I wish I had said yes.

Letter Home, 1920

What I miss most
is the smell of peat-smoke on my bible
before falling into bed,

stinking, silvered with fish.
Lucky we've a proper mattress,
the three of us

head to tail
beneath dailies pasted on the walls
to stem the stench.

Dawn to nightfall, Sundays off –
me and Ceit and Màiri at the farlin,
our fingers bound with flour sack rags,

the cutags' slice, twist, turn
and the guts are in the basket,
the herring in the tubs –

madgies, fulls and matties layered in barrels
packed with salt
that makes our scratches yowp.

Twenty crans a day we clear –
but time wheeches by,
songs rolling over the lines of girls

like the Minch on Claigan bay.
The bosses don't understand our tongue
but on the Sabbath

Reverend MacLeod leads us all in prayer,
Ar n-Athair a tha air nèamh.
Every night I pray for you and *boban*,

for the sheep's good health,
peat for the hearth,
corn and turnips in the ground.

Squeezed between Ceit and Màiri,
my dreams are silver – east coast
sea and sky; the shillings at the end of the season

that will buy us rubber boots
and two fine pots for the croft; the glitter
staring up from all those creels.

Light's Tricks

The sea is ripped green paper
and I am full of longing. Sometimes the sun
is netted and distended on the waves,
held there like a shivering coin.
Sometimes it's a disc of ruched taffeta,
or a small sweet tangerine.

I've never been much good at swimming
but I can keep myself afloat. Further out
the sea is a tabletop of green marble.
A friend invited me to swim and I said no –
too cold this time of year. Truth is,

it's not the freezing temperature I fear
but leaving these comforts behind –
a woollen jacket, gloves, strong shoes;
the giving-up by degrees; loss
a necessary measure of whatever thrill
might meet me there.

A child learns it's not the Sun that moves
but Earth. How do you get your head round that?
Fact is, you don't. You give yourself away
to logic, graphs, and an adult's wiser words.
I think the heart might be like that.

I've loved another man, and then another,
and the drowning and the flight were almost worth it.
Everything has its tipping point. Earth tilts
on its axis and the sun with all its fizzing gases
tilts too, in its own way. Even the green paper
does not sit entirely flat at its torn edges.

The sun has crept from that fin-shaped dip
to the lower headland and its twin face on the sea
has shifted with it. Everything has its place.
Even the tiny fishing boat bobbing out there,
anchored by its shadow, will be steered back
into harbour at the end of the day.

Notes

"Night Walk, Baile Mòr": In memory of the four young men from Iona who died on 13 December 1998 when their dinghy overturned as they were returning home from a night out on Mull.

"Sheela-na-Gig": Figurative carvings of naked women, often positioned over doors or windows to keep away evil spirits, were once part of church decorations across Europe.

"The Dream": On 1 January 1919, HMS Iolaire was bringing servicemen home to Lewis and Harris when it hit rocks yards from shore, drowning 205 men.

"The White Cow": Legend says a cow appeared from the sea during a year of harsh famine. Curiously, the skeleton of a large extinct type of cow known as an auroch was found during recent excavations at the Ness of Brodgar, Orkney.

"A Seat at Cailleach Farm": In Gaelic mythology, the Cailleach ('old woman') is a creator deity as well as a destructive storm hag.

"Letter Home, 1920": 'Herring girls' were employed in all big British ports during the herring boom of the early twentieth century. They travelled down the east coast from Aberdeen to Great Yarmouth, following the shoals as they migrated.

Acknowledgements

I would like to thank the editors of the following journals in which versions of some of these poems have appeared: *Agenda, Gutter, Magma, Mslexia, Northwords Now, Poetry Ireland Review, Orbis, Poetry Ireland Review, Poetry News, Poetry Salzburg Review, Prole, Stand, The London Magazine, The Moth, The North, Stand, Strix, The Frogmore Papers, The Interpreters House,* as well as The Emma Press anthology *In Transit: Poems about Travel, Aesthetica Creative Writing Annual 2020,* and *Coast to Coast to Coast.*

Appreciation and deep thanks go to Roselle Angwin for her insight and guidance during our annual retreats on Iona where many of these poems began their lives, to Bill Greenwell and the participants of his online Poetry Clinic for their invaluable feedback, also Lucy Wadham, my husband Alex without whose support I would be a crazy lady, and my daughters Skye and Gaia.

Prizes

"Passing It On" won 1st prize in the Guernsey International Poetry Competition 2019

"The Lean Years" won 1st prize in The London Magazine Poetry Prize 2018

"Eggs" won 1st prize in the Manchester Cathedral Poetry Competition 2017

"Post Op" won 1st prize in the Poets and Players Poetry Competition 2017

"Angling" (previously "Fishing") won 1st prize in the Prole Laureate Poetry Competition 2016

"Fault Lines" won 3rd prize in Wells Literature Festival Poetry Competition 2019

"The Dream" won 4th prize in the Kent & Sussex Poetry Society Open Poetry Competition 2017 and was commended in the Yeovil Prize 2016

"Eriskay Wives" was runner-up in the Mslexia Poetry Competition 2017

"The last woman born on the island" was highly commended in the Wigtown Poetry Competition 2016 and shortlisted in The London Magazine Poetry Prize 2016

"Letter Home, 1920" was highly commended in the National Memory Day Writing Competition 2017 (Best Poem category)

"Thirty-Seventh View of Mount Fuji" was highly commended in the Ilkley Literature Festival Poetry Competition 2015 and shortlisted in the Wells Festival of Literature Poetry Competition 2015

"Hebridean" was commended in the Winchester Poetry Prize 2016

"Fourteen" was shortlisted for the Keats-Shelley Prize for Poetry 2018

"Instead of gulls" was shortlisted in the Live Canon International Poetry Prize 2020

"Upper Cut" (previously *Cut'n'Dye*) was shortlisted in the Frogmore Poetry Prize 2016

"Revisiting the Island" was shortlisted in The Bournemouth Writing Prize 2022

"Room Six" was nominated for the Forward Prize for Best Single Poem 2018